The Paradoxes of Water

ROD MORAN was born in 1952 in Seymour, a small country town about
120 kilometres north of Melbourne. His father was a professional
soldier who served during the Korean War, and the family moved
between the East and West coasts of Australia over the years as his
postings necessitated.

This was to have a lasting effect on Moran's sensibilities, attuning
him to the oceans, rivers, bush hinterlands and cities he encountered
as he grew on both sides of the continent.

His father's experiences—including his time in Korea and the earlier
loss of his older brother as a POW at the Sandakan death camp in
British North Borneo during World War II—infused Moran with an, at
times adversarial, awareness of profound political and historical issues
to do with the carnage of the 20th century.

A graduate of the University of Melbourne, Moran's first poetry was
published by *The Bulletin* magazine, a key journal in Australian literary
history, when he was just 18 years old. He has had three volumes of
poetry published, *High Rise Sniper*, *Against the Era* and *Listening to the
Train Passing*. His verse has been anthologised nationally and
internationally, including by Oxford University Press.

In addition, he is the author of two substantial works of Western
Australian history, *Massacre Myth* and *Sex, Maiming and Murder*. The latter
was short-listed for the 2003 Margaret Metcalf Award for excellence in
archival research.

Moran is also well-known as the biographer of Tom Gray, a highly-
regarded identity of Aboriginal descent from WA's Pilbara region, killed
fighting pro-Nazi elements of the French Foreign Legion in Syria in
1941. Moran is also a prize-winning journalist.

He has worked as a labourer, school-teacher, full-time union official,
academic, and community newspaper publisher. He is currently literary
editor of *The West Australian*, the capital city's morning daily.

The Paradoxes of Water

SELECTED AND NEW POEMS 1970–2005

ROD MORAN

SALT

CAMBRIDGE

PUBLISHED BY SALT PUBLISHING
PO Box 937, Great Wilbraham, Cambridge PDO CB1 5JX United Kingdom

First published 2005

Printed and bound in the United Kingdom by Lightning Source

Typeset in Swift 9.5 / 13

ISBN 1 84471 108 0 paperback

SP

1 3 5 7 9 8 6 4 2

To my darling wife Lyn, with the splendours of the blue sea-wind in your golden hair, my love—forever.

Contents

Acknowledgments

Almost all of the poems selected here, except for the new verses, were first published in Australia's leading literary journals and newspaper columns over the last 35 years. All are acknowledged with kind thanks.

A number of the poems have been anthologised nationally and internationally, including in *The New Oxford Book of Australian Verse*, edited by Les Murray, and *The Oxford Book of Modern Australian Verse*, edited by Peter Porter.

I also wish to acknowledge Artlook Books, Fremantle Arts Centre Press and Platypus Press, the publishers of my first three volumes of poetry.

High Rise Sniper 1970–1980

Above all to Lyn and Peter

Chemical Worker
For Ron

One day, I said, there will occur
a great scraping out of your gut,
sulphides and the muck of caustic.
(We catch rank eels at the factory step
where our acid kills rich river weed).
A surgeon will scalp your best lung,
a mortician deliver cosmetic lies
to your only funeral: you will smile
like a cheap wreath. He replied:
death weighs heavily upon the living,
it is best to lay dead looking robust.
And recognise this substantial fact:
power breathes from their waking mouths,
(command, complaint, terse demand),
and this pure acid, like some cruel psalm,
gives us daily bread: remember, they too
have a place in the maggot's equation.
Besides, at the last moment I know
that breath is always short: lungs collapse
like anemones choked with oil.
As for prayers: I say them like insurance.

Country Town

A possum skates across
the shimmering street,
finches sizzle in the blackberry.
A koala, evolution's
sleepy dead end,
chews bitter leaves
all day long, dozing
high in the ivory gums.
Crows shimmer green
and black on dead boughs.

Farmers with eyes
the colour of dust,
arms like twisted banksia,
solemn as crows at a carcass,
perch outside the pub,
faces hard against
the granite twilight.
The talk is of fences
and paddock gates.
Utes nuzzle the gutter like horses.

Cross Country

For Jamie

Where the road turns to water,
I sometimes mistake an old tyre
for a wallaby smashed on the road,
butchered by a semi-trailer.
Broken possums look like tyres too,
their inner tubes ripped out,
perishing like rubber in the sunlight.
Occasionally, half a galah flock
is spattered in its own pink
feathers and gore in mad array,
swimming down the highway
like grotesque fish
in the heat's bright lagoon.
Goannas rot in the mirage too,
crushed by a Mack diesel swerved
to scrawl them like red graffiti
emblazoned on the bitumen.
Down the highway's burning gravel
the land's totems lie shattered.
Cross country, where the road
turns to water, I know something
is drowning in its own blood.

Dreaming

In sleep, a claim staked
to rampant drought,
suspicious crows strutting
the cracked sod, a cairn
of old bones and red dirt,
where once ancestral hearts
implored the arid earth.
Strange atavist, my dreamtime
sees distant sheep wade
a torrent of clear heat,
bright bush parrots tear the air
in barbed shrieks, glow
like fanned embers in the afternoon
tinder wind and dry burn.
Ridges float in the amber wash
where, a vivid rainbow,
the Serpent spat a tilted world.
The tribes' artesian blood
stains ancient rock, spinifex.
Some nights a farmer stands
stump-legged in stubble
swelling like a topaz tide,
fingers sifting broken clay.
Beyond the map of taut fences
a black man sings of death,
plaintive, at the fringe of my sleep.

from Suburban Details

1. HIGH RISE SNIPER

Lord of his Babel,
the suburb prone along his sight,
determined the world
must share his dark;
not madness this hatred,
but vengeance for his torment.

He is our mirror, our making,
the logic of our streets.

Each squeezed shot shatters
a glowing window;
light dies, a body slumps,
falls like a question mark.

Sirens, the strutting strobe
goose-steps across the pavement.

Surrounded, he is lord of his tower.
They cannot stop
his final free-fall.

2. SUICIDE POEM FOR THE BUS DRIVER

Half of his face
is in the mirror.

Half an image
of his tired eyes
hangs at the end
of the bus aisle.

One callous pall
of neon light
thrust through
the fractured image.

Outside the cab,
concrete path.
And the last run is
so very lonely.

5. SISYPHUS

He is Sisyphus on the factory floor,
nobody's sweetheart and a slave.
Between shifts he sometimes checks
that the seasons have not ceased,
or watches how a myna bird
dances up a bough. Until his last
time-clocked breath he stoops,
shoulder hard against the day,
and heaves up a crowded hill.
At night in raucous public bars
he rages against the gods.

7. SUBURBAN RAIN

Tonight I am haunted by
this noiseless tracer,
how each day our orbits
spiral towards nothing,
this vertical silence,
and how the planets spin
echoless always. Tonight,
shining streets stretch
the stars at cross-roads,
alleys glow in stellar water
like narrow constellations.
In parallax and silence
the universe eddies,
concentric in a puddle.

from Bass Strait Poems

1. WYBALENA CHAPEL, FLINDERS ISLAND

Developed by George Augustus Robinson
in an effort to save the Tasmanian
Aborigines from extinction.

The chapel ministers to petrels,
a parish of tussock and kelp;
below the dunes, a mass grave
and other accusations:
the rancid huts bulldozed,
clay mounds of tern nests,
guano and dead scrub.

Sea-birds arc half the world to nest here,
eyes bright with constellations,
star-maps, curving water.
The tribes trekked centuries
of ice and rock to arrive, far south,
make fire, camp, and together
dance between gums scaling
cliffs of sheer light.

Instrument of God's love,
Robinson, entrepreneur,
harsh hand of History
and invented fate,
hurried them deathward:
graves mapped, named,
a bucolic Belsen.

The granite remembers,
night-birds, wallaby,
the sand knew their soft tread;
their songs return in bird throats,
well up through the wide
clear rapids of silence.

The chapel stands empty with wind.
Imagination bends like light
to recreate what is gone.
Lizards congregate against the moss,
invisible, always present.
Finches hymn in the rafters.

2. KELP FARMERS

Like sea-birds they scan the distance,
pray for storms.
Stranger than Druids,
they worship the gales
that rip the kelp from deep under.

On the beach, enigmatic gulls,
they kick aside the lesser weed,
lean into the wind;
talk in metaphysics
of kelp, delivering tides,
a litany of tempest.

I ask of boats swamped
by winds from the Pole,
of men lost in the gales,
washed tangled in kelp
like spars on the shore.

They return silence,
their eyes circles of stormy distance.

On the beach a crew of gulls
awaits another harvest.

4. INLET, FLINDERS' ISLAND

The water's history is etched
in tide levels on rock and estuary mud,
beached clams, mussels, crab husks.
Lava hissed boulders round as planets
into the boiling sea; waves crack
like granite against them still.
Shearwaters burrow the tussock,
and this mankind, recent arrival by carnage,
brief as a green lizard on a rock,
reaches towards earth's core
to snap their tense necks.
They are how I have read geography
moulds a man's heart, how history's
nightmare weighs on our daily brain.
On the beach the men are furtive:
great migrations swirl inter-hemisphere,
high above their heads, small birds
have Polar bearings and bright lichen
weathers an epoch of storms; fishermen,
legacy of sealers' carnal havoc,
they know the sea is guilty of nothing,
scuff cuttle and kelp in meditation,
dark boatmen, haunted.

5. BEACH WALK, APOLLO BAY

The bay shines like purple slate,
beached hulls and dune wood,
the sea belling fathoms of brass air,
an amber distance scything
water and sky in its bright curve.
The world gathers itself like this
against human designs, or so it seems:
sand and tide, storms, gull-flight,
the long migrations, dune-wind.
Afternoon, and the water swells
gold as molten glass, the Strait
a tangle of light and dead ships,
the coral skulls of drowned men
ephemeras, feed for polyps.
Ebb, lap, a long surge of wind
through the salt scrub, terns poised
against the slight breeze; lap, ebb,
my steps washed rhythmically
from the ancient sand.

Gardener

For Lyn

She keeps churning the dark loam,
a brown marl of rind and green scrap.
A fertile love tenders trees, bright shrubs,
the dank silt that worms chew and air.
Days of fern-light and dirt she bends
to raise, times later, new greenwood,
or hang, triumphant, a basket blooming
bright to hover like a prism refracting
the cool scent of violets and mossy soil.
Renoir splashes light from leaves like lace.
She shapes sod towards new greenness
where birds will balance and cluck monologues.
Years on, someone will sit, shaded,
and, like her, paint a nurtured world.

Ghosts

For Stan

About five kilometres out
they first insist a presence,
(the sun's frost on late poplars,
evening skeletal between bough
and the frozen humus).
The last logger died in '56,
crushed shapeless under a ton
of slaughtered lemon gum.
His memory is a forgotten plaque
pinned to a dead tree.
The old pub has endured:
you sense them there too,
bellying the hard-wood bar,
yarning, snowed in forever.
Others fossick the green river,
sluice the silt of their days,
quartz, the hard melted snow.
Here, shadows are cold granite
gouged by a torrent of years.
About five kilometres out
I first felt their presence,
(ibis ghosting chrome dams,
the cold sheen of sun on the bracken,
an absence against the landscape).

Kampuchea

As in Bruegel's *Massacre*,
the Innocents lie dead in the village square.
Here, only the snow is missing.
How to assert love against such negations:
a Spanish Duke, swaddled in power,
supervising the slaughter; or this young girl
dying bloated by the road,
eyes like bright mirrors, and in her stare
the whole earth burning.
Art cannot push the boundaries of suffering back;
it can only record the dark beasts living,
prophesy the burnt jungle's return,
made green by her many-million bones.

Rabbits

For Lyn

Travelling overland
past the salt marsh inlets,
relentless semis
thundering through the night.
I prayed the rabbits
thumping wet against the chassis
would not disturb your sleep.
I heard them squeal
blood above the engine's scream.
Hurtling across dark flats,
herons like ghosts
stilt-legged on the salty mud,
distant tail-lights
iridescent rabbit eyes.
Stopping to refuel
I felt their accusing presence,
their silence like wind
through the tussock,
rabbits, side-ways staring,
taking my measure.

Remembering Greg

Tonight, I think of Greg,
who is dead (a small paragraph,
page 12 *The Daily Telegraph*),
his brain in hieroglyphics
across the wall of a Sydney flat.
My attention cleaved between
TV and a book of poems,
he returns a decade later.
We wrote pamphlets in the Ocean Beach Hotel,
fought for Vietnam in the public bar,
the sun a blaze of sand, blinding,
the sea strumming our lives.
Outside the glass, the long slow
tides of ocean and time,
messages cast and drifting still,
or broken on the generous rocks
of a wider disbelief.
Tonight, his presence spans
ten years between this TV ad
and a poem I cannot fathom,
all his strength straining at the trigger.

Silos

Druid priest to ghosts of wind,
the moon performs its ritual rise,
a forest of fossiled trees in array,
like monks strung in procession.
There, above the green-black gums,
this moment forever in silhouette,
silos rise like Stonehenge.

Swan River

Years ago, where the river hugged
wide around the old red brewery,
I watched sombre swans glide
still and gentle as autumn,
immaculate shadows that mocked
evening's quiet dark flung wide
like a sly silent net: they would
billow their slim black wings
and lick the last trembles of light
from the smooth water.

Now all the river swans are gone.
We struggle to recreate the form:
imagine the meaning of feathers.
A silent shape lies broken between the reeds.

Evening billows wilful and precise:
across the taut water neon spirals
a sharp and frenzied symmetry of light.

Yesterday, tangled in mud and scum,
I found a faded piece of red beak.

The rest I could not imagine.

Travelling

Radio static spits against the glass
like rain, a torrent of darkness
spinning startled 'roos across the deadly light,
sprinting them deep into the black
wake of bush and silence.
A song fades in, then out,
like a slow-motion parrot across the high-beam.
Towards the Alps, a road-side café,
a reprieve, time to meditate
on a burger and chips,
or ponder the journey's end:
sign-posts glow a moment in the speeding light,
breaking moths against the globes.
Truckies sip bitter coffee,
argue the road ahead, skids-spots, police,
the return haul, eyes gunning
a wedge of light into oblivion.
Pushing on, beer-eyed,
each destination receding darkly,
flying down the lit tunnel of head-lights,
telling myself I am going somewhere,
that tomorrow I will arrive.

Against the Era 1982–1988

To Stanton Halik, in appreciation of dialectic, and in memory of John Kellock, leader, La Vida Jazz Band.

"The subject . . . I think, of every possible
form of poetry is the human condition."
–EUGENIO MONTALE, 1972

from Against the Era

AGAINST THE ERA
In memory of Eugenio Montale, 1896–1981

What can save us in this time
from our many forms of death,
the Gestapo of all perfect wisdom
and agents of the hidden hand?

Imperfect love might suffice, or
counterpoint to each human form,
the sun that sheens to amber slate
along the sky's sloped scree.

Let us make a deathless pact
with the beauty of inert rock,
the grain of wind that benignly quarries
starkest stone for its hard truth.

BOLSHEVIK CHIC

They sit inside their cafes talking,
the sun outside is full and clear;
the topic is their latest insight,
and flows like wine and German beer.

They sip their coffee very loudly,
chat of their new relationship,
French film and other arty issues,
consuming shrimp with minor dip.

Their dress is kind of urban funky,
with specs that turn their eyes like cats,
and in the hollow of their gossip,
you'll hear their tales of terrace flats.

They invoke Trotsky after entrée,
discuss his handbooks page by page,
(dwell awhile on their own oppression,
being trapped on a handsome wage).

So, in between the renovations,
smart real-estate, hip custom jeans,
these *nouveau chic* proletarians
storm the high turrets of their dreams.

ELEGY

In memory of Ron Moran, 1924–1945,
2/4th Machine Gun Battalion 2nd AIF,
died Prisoner of War, Sandakan death camp,
British North Borneo.

I

Only days beyond
your twenty-first year,
the war's last beat,
the whole Earth bleeding,
you ended where death
hung across bleak wire,
barbs of historic light
cutting silhouettes
on the innocent morning.
(No, your death is a rumour:
we guess sadly where
your last teeth smile).

II

The torpedo crushed flesh,
the frail steel of boys,
decked out those dark soundings
with skull and white limb.
A past and future fodder-type,
young to an ancient war,
your cause a vague laurel,
sharp-shouldered, keen as hope,
Perth blacked out against
a too-far black horizon.
To survive then was your
young death's beginning,
transported where: Siam,

Borneo, the Burma line,
long stints of labour unto death?
Have you gone to old bones
in the jungle's green snare?

III

Your mother survives still,
her voice thin as a telegram:
two husbands, sons, two wars,
she lives despite the era,
your memory grim jetsam.
Your generation haunts
its own mothers always.

We talk of you;
there is much not said,
you smiling yellowed
and young on the dresser,
me trying to imagine
you like your brothers,
trying to pay homage.
The afternoon sun shone
bayonets in the window.

Thirty-six years on
she still mourns,
lost in a deep quiet,
a grief that is all
she does not utter.
We pool words over tea,
you waiting in the wings
like distant tragedy.
Your entrances are various.

LEADERS

Some will arrive there on the steel flat sea.
Black barges of calculated iron
will unload by moonlight the common troops:
their leader will be a proud just Lion.

Still others will spin down the lunar air
of politics, sounding shrill words of peace.
In smart cafes by wine-light they will sell
kind schemes: their loved leader will be a Thief.

And the keen Liar will invade by ruse
the full hearts of the grim well-intentioned,
as they clamour for the Lion's good might,
ignoring all the Thief never mentioned.

Liar and Thief and the proud just Lion
will construct their usual walls and wire:
the Liar will govern, the Lion stalk,
the Thief will cruelly mock the buyer.

MASS MEETING

Here we all are gathering in this place,
where passions can well and belief run free;
(there's a young Lenin with a Testament,
in truth a bit-player who hopes to be).

I look at the meeting and try to think
about the issues we're here to address;
outside the rain stammers insistently,
wind scatters leaflets in a cold caress.

For many there is meaning here, and more,
for others the pulse of true History flows;
I smile to a friend who quietly jokes.
All across the tense hall a silence grows.

The debaters rise in a solemn line,
a collective mind is asked to respond;
a vote is taken as the hall seeps cold:
the gathered all warm in a mythic bond.

We spill like chatter out across the street,
(young Vladimir struts, noble as a bust),
we occupy a dozen public bars —
the talk is of football, of Art and lust.

And love, always love, for her and the Tribe,
for all that is good in our gracious eyes.
Rain blurs our vista from the bar-room sill,
and we huddle closer as the fire dies.

Poem on the Anniversary of Pablo Neruda's Death

> The poet gives us a gallery full of ghosts
> shaken by the fire and darkness of his time.
> —NERUDA, *Memoirs.*

Fresh from the rich lyric of your memoir,
the fire and shadow of your life's time,
I imagine you climbing the granite heights,
Macchu Picchu, dreaming the verdant
Chilean forests, reciting in the miners' camps;
seeker in the hills of shattered Spain
in search of Lorca's murdered bones,
carrying in the splint of your ribs
your own broken heart for the world;
singing of the mouths stuffed with clay,
throats torn on the bloody scarp of power,
frigid stars blinking like distant pity,
the serrated ice on the snow shroud's hem
like knives in the eyes of generations.
At Isla Nega your plundered home
is silent, a spoked wreck weaving wind.
The black bootprints of a shrill mob
are stained deeply on your splintered door.
Where have all your mermaids gone,
their eyes full of the sea's splendour?
Your windows were like sheets of sail
breasting the planet's fierce dark winds.
In Valparaiso there wafts the spume
of poems burning like heaps of leaves.
O Pablo, each day recalls someone's death.
History gathers them like black beads.
This one is yours. Tonight the moon
spiders down the web of barbs,
seeps through the perished wood of barracks,

the ocean a seamless silver glaze,
illuminates your cherished nation,
its hopes strangled in an umbra where,
someone reads, persistent as love,
poems majestic as condor wings.

Politics

These are the patterns shaped like blades,
the cuneiform script of hatred,
the sickle-syntax of the mullah.

They are also the fetid swamps,
the snake-groves and the quicksand,
the rank waters that rust thought and care.

See how they strut with their wide plans
the cold quarries of the builders?
(Stone skids on flesh to raise a pyramid).

I know a man who once witnessed
a miracle of the *politia*:
whole families wafting up chimneys.

Spring Premonitions

1

The sky is like bruised camellias;
somewhere, a storm commences.
I think of the world's broken flesh.
(Birds dart like dark bullets;
a sparrow ricochets through
a skein of smouldering petals).

2

In deep winter I often doubt
this beginning again, and again,
how the blossom slowly happens,
floral light budding pink hands
palming high currents of air.
Leaves clatter like gunfire.

3

Bark moss dries; these boughs
dream varied pods and fruit.
The wind wears a pure colour,
the rich spectrum of berries.
At this moment's resurrection,
other trees burn in dead streets.

4

Today I saw four birds brawl
in a mesh of budding frond,
a careful anger and benign history.
Spring, the surge of true sap.
But the dying light is ambiguous,
the whole world transformed.

STAFFROOM

Some doze in the thin autumn light,
gathering dust like unread books.
Earnest talk ravels its tight knot
around real estate; furtive looks
are exchanged between those two there
(all know why, it's a broken code).
Some laughter erupts, then dies off.
She talks about the latest *Mode*.
What can be said here where learning's
a rumour of chalk, understood
by whom and when? Ideas are
like grains of dirt on perished wood.
The cups are disposable foam.
He complains that the milk is blown.

Understanding Hegel/TV

I have turned the kettle up;
a charming midget descends
dangling from a fake balloon.
He peddles used cars using
his perfect speech impediment.
A copywriter commits atrocity.
I almost believe each proposition:
for a split second all is clear,
like evaporation from glass.
(Reason lies groggy in the corner).
The old kettle hisses wetly
above the midget's hot-spiel.

*Is this also the Absolute
working its way through History?*

UNEASY BELLS

Uneasy bells ringing,
concentric in my brain.

What do they foretell,
question or announce?

No cathedrals spire song
high above this ground.

Is it the silver gull's howling,
the sea's metallic boom?

Uneasy bells chime,
reverberate and swell.

What is this rising coda?
The wind brims dark with sound.

Waffen Skins, MELBOURNE

They strutted towards
the Jewish quarter,

dark stubble like wire
on their oblate skulls,

chains and razors
bright as medals.

Their black leathers shone
like cold gun-metal,

Waffen Skins tattooed
on their foreheads.

The old Jews strolled home,
stoically knowing,

(wrists indelible,
stained deep blood-blue)

even decades on,
a world's curve away,

some nights the barbed stars
turn yellow early.

WAYS OF LAUGHING

Laughing like a lost cause,
conscious of its fate:
(a refugee from Time's regime,
the circled face of clocks).

Laughing like a small bird
that skips between the bars:
(the jailer who deserted,
the architect who failed).

Laughing: a geometer
who crossed parallel lines:
(death in heaven, pain in joy,
an IOU in the Promised Land).

Laughing like a fisherman
jagging tuna in the desert:
(he hauls shoals from the dunes,
but they won't believe his eyes).

Laughing like an immigrant
who walks on broken glass:
(the jokes on him, he knows it,
the last colony of his hopes).

Laughing: an intellectual
with his first taste of power:
(the wires in his kind brain
are giggling with barbs).

Laughing like a woman
whose marriage is a crime:
(broken cheeks, livid eyes,
face lovely as a vow).

Laughing like a torturer
injecting a vaccine:
(the lie of Utopia,
the tetanus of perfection).

Laughing like the Killing Fields,
the guffaw of a bullet:
(a child in the mud, the mirth
of wind like lost voices).

WIRE

Consider the significance,
for a modern metaphysics,
of the honed nettles of wire.

Its coiled scrolls of barbs
ornament the mind's cage,
fence the sacrificial pit.

The speeches of important men
glisten with its polished barbs.
Wire is the claw of power.

Wire conducts the lightning
of all dominant ideas:
husks of people hang from it.

Try arguing for the perfect State
while not losing a sad count
of the dead in their electric yards.

No informed dissertation
on cause, effect and induction,
time and space and sense perception

can ignore the logic of wire,
the semantics of taut steel.
Power's teeth are braced with it.

It clearly marks the perimeters
of permitted doubt and knowledge.
(The piano version strings gibbets).

Imagine two philosophers
disputing, a skull-white beach,
a sea of wire and razored tides.

You will observe how they tread
through the stark skeletal maze,
trying to establish a beach head.

from Theorems of the Senses

An Ecology

The wind-mill's rusted skeleton
propped on its own thin shadow.

Twenty ivory egrets roosting
the silver dam's ochre ridges.

The day's balance consisted in:
birds, water and two artefacts.

BUTTERFLY HOUSE

On the hot wet heavy humid air,
flood of the rainbow's iridescence,
they hang like amber kites,
or delicate luminous shrapnel.
In this simulated jungle dome,
butting against a green glass sky,
(a Blue Ulysses seeking home),
others, indigo and shimmering,
are velvet shards on the damp thermal,
kaleidoscopic fragile light,
petals ablaze like red sulphur,
a silent geometric dapple,
(rhomboid topaz, triangular black).
I imagine Da Vinci strolling here,
subverting the airlock, freeing them,
a perfect design crystallising
a jewelled molecule in his mind.

MOVING HOME

Digging the forgotten strata,
finding again parts of myself,
(prints, notations, dusty letters,
ideas, fragments on a shelf).

I sift the dross, the chunks of years,
hear my footsteps chime in the hall,
relinquish what I had cherished,
burn old papers, wash down the walls.

The lemon tree, as ever, blooms
outside the lounge-room window pane.
The boughs are laden down with fruit.
The wind pauses, then gusts again.

This leaving is like a return
to where I had been once before;
(a book that I had loved with passion
is stacked with junk upon the floor).

Outside the house, the wind moves on.
I excavate, read with a frown
an arrival piece I'd written,
laying the deep sediments down.

THE SCHEME OF THINGS
For Lyn

When I emerged from the quetzel sea,
it was the burning granules of sand,
the plumes of light and refracted glare.
How could I regain those violet depths,
beckoning tides and the limestone forest,
the caress of waves like peacock tails?

When I descended from the purple
quartz of sky, it was the turning hawk
hanging on the puppet chords of time,
the stone air shimmering from its wings,
the flat seismic landscape expectant.
I was in its eye like a fleeing form.

And when along the compass of thought,
skid of words, sharp turn of memory,
I drove across this verdant image,
the green-wet, square magma hills distant,
an indigo haze like hard black bread,
it was then what I had forgotten:

your face amongst the sunflower dials,
the sulphur dawn, a white froth of birds
rising like bubbles from sodden trees,
as if all of life was a retrieval,
a dredging the strata of loss and meaning,
for beauty, origins, counterpoints to time.

SLEEPLESS

My skull is a clutter
of night debris:

nearby a car skids
on the dew-wet dark.

Cicada chant,
train-clack and thought.

Even the moon stains
through my closed lids,

bright as a flood-light,
barbed in silver,

climbs a scaffold
of black trees

framed in my window,
refracted in blinds.

I'm a refugee
from myself tonight,

queuing at the border,
desperate to cross.

from West Coast Suite

MEDITATIONS OF A FISHERMAN

1

I awoke tonight, as if someone had called,
a voice, a clutter of gulls,
left my bed as if to answer,
black sea-birds skimming silhouettes
like bats across the lunar haze.
All night the churning brine had billowed,
the moon's blue barge a lumber of stars
drifting in the ocean's midnight tow.
Even at this remote sounding
these human labours strain against
the sibilant tide of night-worn wind.
From the harbour's black a cray boat
prows the fin-like curve of swell,
its lights a tiny constellation,
like flares tattooed upon the water,
plying fragile decks, weeks out
in shark and crustacean zones,
crewed by small aims, passing lives.
I woke tonight, gull-chant and sea wind,
alone in a dark gale of my years.

2

In visions that are the clearest nights,
I have seen the small terns leave again
to fly beneath other glowing worlds,
scud sleek across an Arctic plain,
pure dunes of ice like frozen sand,
the wind-filled silence that spirals,
cold and star-laden on the sea.
You are a point of reference that calls
like tussock, the clean fragrant drifts.
Was your face the moon tonight,
flecked by a dream of returning birds?

3

My love, I haul against the slub of nets,
seek moorings safe from the claw of storms,
an embrace against all entropy.
Tonight, I cast out once more
to basket finned and spiny herds,
a light blinking from the rocky point,
towed by moon and spinning waters,
my sure elements my lust and love,
the pure and gorgeous salt of you,
these tides guiding my wearied hull,
gulls calling reconciliation.

Night Fishing
For Neil Kimpton

Their lamps glaze white paths
narrowly on the bay's dark circle,
spears like sharp flutes in the wind.
Two figures wade an enigma of shoals,
hours probing the translucent water,
unseen currents swirling sand
from beneath soft, cray-flesh feet.
Small squid skid away just beyond
the green marble of their light;
fish are fluorescent darts blurring
a moment under fractured water.
They wander in the night's black swell,
judging refraction and eddy, guessing.

RETURN
For Lyn

My dreams come back, suddenly clear,
and the loveliness of the world.
Am I absent from myself so often
that these liquescent scans of blue,
(pelicans scudding the taut calm,
tides and the wild light), appear again
as if my eyes had never framed them?
And then there is you, hair streaming sun,
watching ibis graze small pools and sky.
By all this familiar beauty I'm stunned,
my dreams returned, and I to myself.

RETURNED TO MY CHILDHOOD LUNAR RIVER

Returned to my childhood lunar river,
I watch again nets sieving the dark,
small lamps like halos on the night's shore,
gold angels of fish in the circled light.
Felt the gentle scarf of a tepid wind,
brine satin and the images of perfume,
peppermint trees and the clean fragrant sand,
wavelets like facets of an intricate story.
Saw the sleek-leaning geometric yachts,
the phosphorescent confetti of stars
scattered across the river's black shoulders,
drank the music and murmurs of the water,
a sparse map of buoy lights signalling dimly
hidden channels, the snags of returning,
reclusive river birds with their secrets.
I arrived at the dazzle of moorings,
long fragile spars of pier light trembling,
the violet water like a tapestry tale,
a white and luminous sandstone moon,
performing its indelible rites and eddies,
liquid moon, mineral as memory,
the shining needle-neck of a cormorant
unpicking the shallows of bright darting fish,
scarves of lavender strewn across the bay,
sequins of purple stitched to the shadows,
boats embroidered like flecks on the water,
plumes and pennants of high cirrus swirling.
And a gentle dapple of drifting swans
coloured the litmus of recollection,
reconstructing my invisible heart,
the rich silence like a question's answer.

from The Lazarus Poems 1990–

A Western Front Vignette

Lazarus went seeking a saloon-bar of heroes,
those who know the crucible.
Met a man who wandered from the smoke,
like a tattered ghost at Passchendaele,
mustard searing spit and flesh.
Compared stories, shaking crabbed hands.
Spoke of sunlight sparking cavalry lances,
horses thundering to the crest, riders calling
Les Boches, ils est fini . . . unaware
of machine guns beyond the green hummock.
The only survivor was Lazarus,
and a bewildered horse he rode to the village,
the sky turned black as peppercorn.

Fishing With Pythagoras

Lazarus swaddled his pallid skin
in rags of darkness and lunar-brine,
perched at the end of the perished jetty,
the moon pinioned in his white eyes,
a still point around which he turned
all night, pondering beginning
and end, two egrets wading
yellow moon-light by the ferry pier.
Pythagoras fished, and described
the perfection of circularity,
telling Lazarus of pure concentrics:
no beginning, no end, each in the other,
casting his line on the glazed river,
counting shimmering circles, watching
night-herons tow a red morning on their wings,
returned from the far side of the water.

Lazarus and the Hiroshima Incident

A Pale Rider cantering.
An apparition from policy's forge,
rivets of equations and high paradigms,
the sun searing a pure nothingness,
the black steed's ionospheric breath.
Lazarus wandered a blitzed world,
the wrecked city a swathe of silence,
the florid flesh of infants dissolving,
like anemones on a summer beach,
parents drinking fall-out from the river.
Death is truly a moment of light.
Other incidentals impressed him too.
I have seen the Apocalypse, and it works.

Lazarus Considers the Gulag

Their veins ached with permafrost
the impossible distance a serration of firs,
barbed dunes of ice and bolted floes,
the Arctic an attainable death.
Lazarus watched a feeble sun
spider through frigid traceries,
weaves of wire skeined with snow,
razored blue with cold flame.
At night, planks snapped like gunfire.
Some wrote letters to a memory,
hope an unattainable state,
and the greatest moral virtue.
Later, the whole universe thawed,
and sweet water seeped from rock.
Bedraggled, some returned to the old cities,
their ruins gaunt as corpses.
They were not recognised,
and nobody called them from their caves.
Lazarus asked a mother to kiss her son,
but she wept and said nothing.

Lazarus Ponders the Moon Further

It took my journey through death,
and its blackly endless hinterland,
to realise the moon's utilitarian face:
it should be an emblem in your eyes,
like a lantern for the darker corners
of town, the labyrinth's rooms:
those umbral corridors of life
wherein lurk what should be noticed
before it notices you, like an ambush.
And, after use, return it to the sky,
near the glorious Pleiades,
and let it dazzle time, beautifully.

Lazarus Returns to a Metropolis

Young Lazarus has returned, again,
haunted by questions: *Where was I*
in all of that wine-black darkness?
A memory without texture or content.
The wind loiters in cold alleys,
with questionable intent,
the junkies' veins singing.
The street's kingdom prepares its laughter.
(What good comes of the gusting grit
and invective of shrunken minds?)
In their shining glass zeniths,
slick-haired clerks, wax-winged angels
of the humming room and screens,
watch the print-out for clues.
His press conference founders
for want of definitive answers.
In the scuffling city squalid gulls
watch him from their smug gutters.
The wind mocks his sobbing.
His clothes are loose-fitting,
musty, and out of date.

Lazarus Sang His Mythos Nightly

Lazarus sang his mythos nightly.
It tasted of the sea and laurel leaves,
dust of granite, musk light of dawn,
a perfume of all the terrains he's known:
ether of the chromium wards,
cordite, mud and marl of bone.
His song embodied rare knowledge,
a theme awesome as light-years.
But who would hear his haunted voice,
a choke of echoes from the high-rise,
the shimmering night's violet tattoo
like a stain on the humid tenements?
What to do but sing, and listen
to *Judas Priest*, *The Grateful Dead*,
watching *Tombstone Territory* on TV,
Gunsmoke and *The Bounty Hunter*,
reruns of all the old shoot-outs
and their melancholy theme songs?

Lazarus, Sleepless

Lazarus wandered the slumbering city,
trailed an ether of stinging doubt
in his wake: *What if immortality*
is all there is? Is this the afterlife,
after all, and these my just rewards?
Sat by the jet river, watching stars
flame like molten glass, pondering
the colour of eternity, the moon's pyre
burning between black buildings.
Met Plato, lurching out of a nightclub,
who said: *Lazarus, you are only*
a shadow of your real self.

The Dead of the Seven Seas

Lazarus weighed the ballast of their bones,
singing a dirge to their memory.
His voice was like sonar seeking an echo.
A rainbow of fish stained skull and socket,
azurite and amber in the drench of light.
He saw sailors strewn in shattered patterns,
like fragments of song and forgotten prayers,
anonymous as molecules, shards
in ravines of the South China Sea,
the granite-black ice of the Arctic.
Steel hulls harbour their trapped tapping,
a Morse like bubbles in the tonnage of water.
None ever returned, though voices called,
waiting by the sea's cave-riddled shore,
each night birdless and wind-swept.
Lazarus watched fishermen sail out,
engines fading beyond the lime-stone bluff,
their lights a vague stipple on the darkness.
Am I the only one who has come back?

Listening to the Train Passing (1988–94)

For Chay Moran, face like an orchid, in her tenth year to heaven
by the Indian Ocean, these poems for later

A Memoir of Birds

The rainbows of silk threaded
through the Cape Lilacs were lorikeets,
sulphur bangles on their throats,
wings tie-dyed with green and purple.
They dined there all day on split berries,
until night poured black vino and ice
in a deluge through the boughs.
I don't know when I first noticed birds.
Perhaps it was climbing the jacaranda
lining the driveway of my childhood home,
the family Chev mottled lilac.
I'd float in an aromatic water
of bloom clusters fragrant as musk,
propped like a vane in a smooth fork
and watch cormorants fly to the river.
(I imagine the same mystery of wind
tugged at Da Vinci's elbows,
pondering a luff of gulls in the harbour).
From those trees I also saw pelicans
spiral slowly down hot afternoons
of blue and shimmering condensations.
A friend told me the pigeons there
were flying-rats, balloons of vermin.
But what I recall most about them
was the sun flaring purple fire
around the neck of my mate's homing-bird,
iridescent feathers singed to a glow,
like the brocade of my mother's party dress,
as if the bird had swallowed an ember.
I recall finches like confetti,
a palette of kingfishers dappling
the dam near my uncle's orchard,
silver-eyes plundering our loquat tree,
gargling the fruit's delicate nectar.
Or perhaps the initial bird I saw

[69]

was that cinnamon harrier crucified
on a barbed fence in the wheatbelt.
Its splayed form haunted my entire holiday.
But possibly, the very first one
was the mynah-chick I found
while harvesting peaches in Monbulk,
a fragile windfall panting at the sun.
It was covered with soft amber quills,
its eyes like two small wells of sky,
wings tiny boomerangs of gristle,
matted with a smooth flecked down.
Its tiny body shivered, expectant
with its own enormous existence.
I knew it would die, but climbed the tree,
the fledgling trembling near my heart,
and placed it in its nest—
thinking, as only a child could, that
it would be better if the bird was someway
towards the clouds before it did.

Aldo the Limeburner

Aldo the limeburner stokes his kiln
all night, its aura the colour of mortar.
It humbles blocks of stone to powder.
His technique is two millennia old,
a dextrous line from Carthage.
Lives ago, he built Imperial quarters,
walls at the exotic limits of Empire.
Aldo's eyes are crimson at their rims,
like small salt-pans seen from a plane,
and his mouth grates with lime.
His hair is stiff with peroxide marl.
His white hands, worn hard and smooth,
repeat gestures that are chisel edged.
The iced beer his dusty wife delivers
flushes his gums like cold acetylene.
Some afternoons he becomes an outcrop,
a stony and magical transformation,
white and weathered amidst the banksias,
levitating on shining thermals.
Birds navigate by him, perch on his lips,
dive for glittering lizards that bask
in his parched erosions and mossy clefts.
Today, he ponders Ovid's poems, heat
seeping from the kiln like sweat,
recites them in cadences of gravel.
Considers his banishment by the sea,
on the margins of a modern suburb,
where maps turn to simmering bush,
flecked by gullies and chalky scarps,
Scythia, Perth, the dazzling desert,
skies embellished with eagle-forms,
a sea-wind skeined by kiln smoke
the colour of lemons and marble grit.
Aldo's sledge shatters a caustic block,
as a silver Boeing arches overhead.

He fires the oven in a cool twilight,
stands back, hands on his rocky hips,
birds poised on his jutting elbows,
face grooved like slate and flushed with fire,
an enigmatic life entailing
all the obscure and hard efforts of building.

An Effect of Black Cockatoos

Early evening, and black cockatoos
cartwheel noisily above my house,
as if some riotous spirit-hand
had spun them at cacophonous angles.
At times they dance a surreal flamenco,
dizzy in the casuarinas, beaks like castanets,
a crescendo black as polished leather.
They scour the sky with iron wings,
in search of seeds and pods to strip,
hissing with the static of existence,
eyes electric, red as novas.
Their screeching is a zinc nail
scraped across the day's glassy-blue.
Far-off, they are a scatter of poppy seed
gusted on a darkening wind.
Tonight, my blood is feather-black,
my throat like the shining birds',
full of kindred sobs and sadness.
Some evenings I evaporate on wings,
scud and thermal in a warp of dreams.
They whirl their vortex at my ear,
the long call of grief against time.
Lately, I have seen them tumble
and cry across an orange moon.
They melt into the black margins,
trailing their corrugated voices,
a fading flutter of tin-foil sound.
It washes up in shimmers and shards
on the lake's opposite shoreline.
Night rises from the water's penumbra,
artesian, immense in its own image.
The birds skid across a flint-black sky.
What zodiac is coded in their brains,
their songs a gravel of lunar noise,
wings star-pocked and ragged aerofoils?

Their intention tonight is to shred
the kernel of a constellation or two,
leaving a scatter of smaller planets
embering on a bare horizon,
like gutted cone-husks from the pines.
They arc along the edges of my sleep,
trapeze insanely across the Milky Way,
eroding and gnawing at the moon,
until all that is left is a din of shadows.

Kettle Baroque

When I burnt the copper kettle dry,
it flecked cinnamon and pearl,
cooling to hues of trout-skin,
a baroque landscape stippled violet,
and the umber of river water.
Sometimes, art is a beautiful fluke.

Listening to the Train Passing

Grunting and pushing its years
along the old suburban track,
the faded locomotive coughs
a rasping coal-dust throat,
past the lush deserted orchard.
Here, roads and the last houses
scatter like wet and fallen leaves
at the frayed limits of the city.

Further down the curving line,
the map of known destinations,
the granules of its voice transform:
they become a solemn fog-horn,
intoning across the sodden air.
So distant from the empty sea,
this plaintive haunting threnody.

And when its last long trumpet
has faded through the early mist,
with silence hanging from the trees,
I stand in my small space of time,
stained by a dark and seeping sense
of irretrievable loss: not of trains,
but of forms that cohere the world.

Until I notice the pure orbs
and boughs of returning fruit:
mandarins in their amber garb,
like meditating masters
pondering on the sky's taste,
the permanence of all that passes,
how the roots of this olive grove
are watering in Ionia.

Marc Chagall by the River

The yachts are like sleek Cadillacs
finning through the afternoon mirage,
silver and attractive as legal tender.
Terriers are bats flying the skyed water,
where scrailing river birds tumble
like kitchen dishes through the air,
a screeching suburban household brawl,
suspended above the blue currents.
Grand houses perch at the water's edge,
like sumptuous Birds of Paradise.
In clustered clumps like crystal grapes,
the chandeliers of the bourgeoisie
hang in a poise of saffron sky.
The pied cormorant in a clucking priest
lecturing the jetty's cluttered crowd
of oblivious barnacles, solemn gulls.
Or perhaps it is a violin,
resonant with a quaver of warm wind.
Like mailed and scaled mini-gods,
fish swim towards the ice-white moon,
orange sickles of coral-tree blooms
a scatter of Greek fire on the suburbs.
Levitating at the water's carnal edge,
the lust and caress of lapping boat wake,
purple amplitudes of rhythmic water,
two lovers kiss in a tall headstand,
perform a Chagallian Karma Sutra,
the bay like sulphate and blue marble,
an intangible dialectic of pure light,
deep sky in the eye's reflective gaze.

My Grandfather's Narration

*In memory of Bill Moran, 10th Light Horse Regiment and 10th
Field Battery Australian Artillery, winner of the Military Medal
for conspicuous gallantry in the field, Cericy-on-the-Somme,
France, 1918.*

My grandfather was a stable-groom.
He polished his horses' porcelain flanks
like rare black Wedgewood.
He loved their jet and olive eyes,
their gentle eddies and innocence.
While raucous cockatoos plundered
their trough of amber oats,
his mares would whinny in a friendly way,
like simple equine Quakers.
On race days, Belmont by the river,
he'd hose his horses against the heat,
sponging their smooth jarrah necks.
He survived the killing fields of France,
but died later, imperceptibly:
his nightmares stampeding
and flaring in the darkness,
hauling a gun carriage over corpses,
through a viscous marl of mud,
lethal as machine-guns.
It was the shrapnel in his memory:
all around there were dead horses,
like bloated barrage balloons,
alive with the iridescent vapour
of flies and their drone of death,
the eyeless heads of ammunition mules,
their silent horse-mouth grins.
For him, the death of a horse
was an awesome and a tragic thing,
(though he shot his waler in Palestine
to save it from an Arab jockey).
When he died, he was leaving Perth,

for a job with horses in the bush,
his marriage dead in the trenches.
On the swaying train, his heart
paused, then simply stopped.
Horses gazed at him from the paddocks.
Perhaps he was dreaming of a long ride,
beyond the wheatbelt out of Narambeen,
like the one his wartime mate took
on behalf of their generation:
800 miles into the Outback, without a word,
until, one day, he reached a spot,
where an azure distance redefined the world,
climbed down, his horse twitching,
lit a fire while the stars exploded,
and stayed there, forever.

from Retinue for Raoul Wallenberg

MESSAGE TO WALLENBERG

Raoul, I must communicate this to you
across a distance I cannot imagine.
I raise a rumour of your own existence.
Perhaps it will reach at the latitudes
of turquoise ice in the floe-bound harbours,
the long dark days of your body's decay.
I offer it to the shrine of your decency,
your granite love, the tender fear
that is the true core of your courage.
Perhaps it will find you in the black
of your final and indifferent grave.
I forward the doves of light that warm me,
mellow freedom, the coloured song of birds,
magenta blossom like prisms of sun,
all that I can offer from the deep spring
of what I feel for your high grandeur.
And I have to add the saddest facts:
the globe still shudders on its flawed axis.
Disappearance is a mode of being,
and diplomats perfect their falsity.
A dark sea has clawed at the shore of our time.
You are like a rare mitigation.
So I send you all that is most precious:
the limits of small continuities,
these thin threads of language and memory,
and whatever can be woven from them.
I send you the frail letter of our hope.

SOMEONE IS CALLING

From the skull of night
someone is calling.

Sharp angles of rain
pierce a fragile voice.

Through a sable wind,
someone is calling.

Black beaks stud the sky
with wings of lament.

From an iron darkness,
someone is calling.

Through the mesh of power
small words are bleeding.

On the quartz of ice,
someone is calling.

In the deep white nights
they cobble a chorus.

On the stony air,
someone is calling.

Like a cherished hope
their throats make laughter.

In prodigious chains
someone is calling.

Echoes and rumours
break in the basements.

Like an ember of need
someone is calling.

The breath of their plea
splits on the tundra.

Someone is calling.
Someone is calling.

A Twentieth Century Parable

In the cottage of the hangman,
the victims sought refuge.
Out of proven strategy,
he served them scalding wine.

Their trip to his grinning step
was a trudge through cruel snow,
a dark ice of moonlight.
At his generous hearth they slept.

Each died an appointed death.
He kissed the corpses, planting
blue lilies at midnight.
The village wept, without orders.

In the cottage of the hangman,
a scholar was hosted.
He scripted lives for the dead,
eulogising their gallows.

Outside, the snow sang darkly.
He sipped scalding wine.
The generous hearth flickered.
The host measured his shadow.

History Moved Through a Forest at Katyn

Tiny birds simmered
in the freezing air.
Philosophy bled.

Amnesia ambushed
many Professors.
Some recalled rumours.

A thin blue column
of innocent smoke
thermalled towards

a silence of sky,
though the sky saw
all that happened.

Poets disappeared.
Hate wrote a sonnet,
winning a medal.

On this very day,
many fell in love.
Warsaw's heart festered.

Smooth shovels shone.
A billow of voices,
bird-wings exploding.

Dark shapes were moving
in a bony forest.
Orders were obeyed.

A sepulchre of trees,
root, mulch and membrane,
rose from the marrow.

Elsewhere, a clerk shuddered.
The marl of necessity.
And History moved on.

* Early in World War II, the Red Army massacred the entire Polish Officer
Corps in a forest near Katyn. The Soviets blamed the Nazis. Since 'glastnost'
the Russians have admitted guilt and had the mass grave exhumed.

The Yanchep Bonfire Raves

RECALLING A RAVE AROUND THE FIRE
WITH ANTHONY LAWRENCE

From the enclave of our fire,
flames flared topaz and stellar-rose.
A star-shot sea darkness lapped
light-years, the shoreline of planets.
We stared into the face of God,
which was the form the sky assumed,
even to my agnostic eyes,
you forgetting lines from a poem,
the honey beer full of starlight,
the pure lexicon of infinity.
So we consumed more, to find them,
the shining paths to meaning being
diverse and worthy of such effort.
Later, the moon rose with its brand,
white as limestone, burning small clouds
with rainbows at their edges.
Anthony, this is what drives us on:
to reinvent all the poems,
imbibing their sustaining nectar,
heaping a fire against the dark,
to strive to say what cannot be said,
while dying galaxies recede,
the flames declining, heavy with dew,
and our shadows evaporate.

THE GLENN MILLER RAVE

You know, the night Glenn Miller died,
the Rhine was fogged in, and all of Poland,
not a viable target in the scope of Europe.
The Squadron arced home, wheeled over vineyards,
white-marble valleys, above inert towns,
serene as cemeteries in the satin mist.
Droned coldly back towards the black Channel,
their fuselages glinting acetylene-blue.
That was what it was like on the night
Glenn Miller evaporated from the sky.
Have you ever considered how many melodies
he conjured as hymns to the beauty of the moon:
Moonlight Sonata, O! You Crazy Moon,
Bluebirds in the Moonlight, Moonlight Serenade,
Moonlight Cocktail, Polkadots and Moonbeams,
Moonlight Becomes You, all suffused with love?
On the night Glenn Miller disappeared,
moonlight refracted from wing and turret,
flooded the cockpit like a wizard's breath,
flight-gear transformed to luminous zoot-suits,
amber stitched and cut from shining shantung:
the ebullient Squadron in a Conga-line,
hep-cat boys singing and crooning like Bing,
the tail-gunner blowing a golden phrase
on the wild trumpet he kept for comfort
on nights like that above the foggy strata,
propellers strobing moonlight and stars,
alone in his perspex bubble of silence.
That was the situation when, by routine,
bombs were jettisoned over the Channel,
payloads of mayhem shrilly out-of-tune:
and Glenn's plane beneath that lethal rain,
en route to rehearsal in liberated Paris,

a treasure of new melodies in his satchel,
the small craft a double-bass flung at the sky,
the band sipping whiskey and tuning up,
impatient as a rash and roaring to swing,
chirpy Glenn possibly humming *In the Mood*,
hearing Tex Beneke whistling the tune:
the tail-gun trumpeter hitting high C,
boogie-woogie bubbling from New York's clubland,
a jitter-bug lullaby eight-to-the-bar,
the Suzi-Q, lindy-hop, tangos of jazz,
Artie Shaw touring a smouldering Pacific,
and the moon emerging all over Europe.
Apparently, it was like that on the night,
Glenn Miller evaporated from the sky.

RAVING TO KEVIN MURRAY ABOUT HIS LETTERS

I was gently placing frangipani blossom
in a wine glass of dry claret
when your epistle arrived from America.
I had imbibed—I know you won't believe
this—a little too much that day,
and was experimenting to see if wine
would absorb the bloom's exquisite fume.
I'm quietly obsessed with that flower.
(Struth, the things we do for beauty).
You wrote describing the bullfight you saw
in Mexico City: nature versus culture,
you said—and it made me speculate
that perhaps that is what rugby is too,
and politics and post-modern poetry.
You can lose your ears in all of them.
In New York you encountered the girls
of your dreams: pale and intelligent,
students from the Julliard school of Music,
lithe forms from the Jaffe School of Dance.
In their chandeliered studies you spoke
about poetry, jazz, the Carlton Football Club,
telling them how you spent the entire week
standing on 125th Street watching Harlem,
studying Manhattan from the Brooklyn Bridge,
strolling up Fifth Avenue, down Lexington,
drifting through the diamond district,
the cold light sharp with amethyst angles,
chatting with Hassidic Jews, their heritage
of jewels, barbed wire and blue tattoos.
And those intelligent lovelies dubbed you:
the man who did nothing in New York!
Well mate, Philistinism has many forms.
Struth, the things you do for beauty.

Later, after Cajun country, Natchez,
the romantic verandahs of old Key West,
full of cool shadows and clarinet riffs,
you wrote to say that you had paid homage
at Sloppy Joe's, the bar where Hemingway
honed cadences, turning his skin bronze
with booze, the last argument a two-barrelled
harangue against his own desperation,
death like a coke-black marlin bursting the water.
Was the night as pared back as his sentences?
Was it a clean well-lighted place?
Next, you write telling me that you stumbled
on Jimmy Buffet singing *Margaretaville*,
in a Tin-Pan alley for coral-reefer rock.
Kevin, you seek beauty in the manner
Stendhal defined it: as a promise of happiness.
And you know what I think would make you happy?
A retirement to the blue Bahamas,
and a PhD on Jimmy's lyrics.
What is most beautiful in your letters
is a dimension of mind, almost as if,
at their heart, there was a frangipani
floating in a glass of red burgundy,
a chemistry as rich as the ether of thought.
Don't take so long to write next time.

The Hank Williams Rave

Coincidental with the year I was born,
Hank did a deal with his Angel of Death,
reality a boozy barbituate blur.
He got blotto in Toronto, a million tears
in his last nine beers, until they tasted
of indigo wear-from-waiting Blues.
In his first publicity shot Hank sports
a tan fedora with a satin band,
and a silk cravat white as honeysuckle.
He looks like a rockabilly aristocrat,
and appears as if he is trying to smile,
as if his pale lips had tasted a stark grief.
His face is gaunt, delicately young.
I think all those ranting Bayou preachers
conjured so much hell in Hank's heart,
he could only trawl in darkness for poems
at depths where all else was unviable,
(God and the Klan handling snakes on Main St).
He sang about love with a kind of pleading,
his art skeined with a thread of despair:
toured Louisiana, the Grand Ol' Oprey,
white lines chasing him through honky-tonks
mildewed with smoke and raunchy promise:
amphetamine midnights, whiskey afternoons,
whole days of whimpering hallucination,
an alligator-moon stalking the river,
the stars shimmering like semiquavers,
a wife prowling sharp as a racketeer,
love a small royalty less the agent's cut,
Gospel tunes sung all the way to the bank.
His Drifting Cowboy Band crooned how,
when the Angel of Death kissed Hank's lids,
he would have to hire someone to mourn him.

Legend holds he horded beneath his bed
an acetate lode of unreleased tunes.
I bet they were veined with a simple happiness,
too rare and precious to risk the sharing.
In elusive moments I think I've heard them,
behind the plaintive chords and the lyrics of loss:
melodies drenched in the Alabama stars,
sung smiling in a voice jaunty with love.

A RAVE ABOUT NATURE AND HUMAN ARTEFACTS

The way evening rushed to a close down
you would think it was Melbourne, 1950,
the bonfire as chaotic and earnest
as those six o'clock swills.
Have you ever considered this enigma:
the way that nature can suggest
human moods, artefacts and arts,
and vice versa, if you see what I mean?
For instance, have you noticed how,
when the gulls billow over the marina,
summer dawn the colour of ingots,
boat windows flashing like schnapper scales:
how, when the birds deploy the white fuses
of their wings through the hot light,
for a moment they explode like flak,
the glazed air pocked vermilion,
like a jarring still from war footage?
 And how boat hulls, smooth as silver,
imitate the bellies of birds in flight,
while the pelican wearing its silhouette
like a shawl, is a monk at sun-rise prayer?
How yacht sails magically fill
every contour of the wind's colour?
And the way the filigree of refinery lights
burning along the rim of Cockburn Sound,
replicates the net of fluorescence
I hauled from a black backwater
in Albany? No? Stoke the fire then.
Consider what the flames connote.
Notice how the hissing amber embers
are like the resin under Grappelli's nails,
his smooth bow whipping up a hot riff:
you know, when the close-ups on TV

show topaz smoke wafting from his strings,
as if they're on fire, watering his eyes.
Or recall how those red half-moons of carp,
languid emblems on the black water at evening,
transform the lake to a shimmering flag.
I don't want to push the point too far,
but I swear I have heard cool wattlebirds
scat-sing all afternoon to a script of blossom,
conjuring nuances of Georgie Fame . . .
anyway, the evening sure closed down quickly.

THE CHARLIE 'BIRD' PARKER RAVE

Exiting the High Hat's clammy bar,
its air thick with a pepper of gossip,
Bird wandered crying in a moonstruck night,
blowing *Ornithology* at the stars,
(diamond-eyed, quetzal plumed),
his blood-flecked cough an abraded chord:
Miss Heroin hanging from his arm,
the fizz of her kiss on his hungry skin,
the dented moon red as a heated spoon,
Bird hallucinating in the shadows.
The city's jive shone as Moose the Mooche,
lizard-eyed pusher to Charlie's arm,
sold oranges spiked with a sherbet of dope,
juice mellow as the cello of Bird's gold sax.
And all the while Charlie is dying,
a liver soaked too long in the suds of rye,
Miss Heroin's magic like welding-light,
burning in his brain with her lethal flame,
Bird craving her lucent riffs and phrases,
pumping the syringe to sustain a gig,
bartering royalties for one good shot:
blue Bird, yard Bird, dope-fiend, thief,
shooting in the alleys by the moon's spiked eye,
bigamist, conman, street-corner wise—
Bird blowing music like redemptive love.

THE DEAN MARTIN RAVE

When they dimmed the lights in Vegas,
an impromptu salute, the card sharks
and hardened gamblers paused mid-Scotch.
The measures of respect are varied.
Some left small winnings uncollected,
as the moon's neon swept the streets
with a dazed and mournful silence,
the pale desert like an unfurled lily.
As the city's fluorescence fell away,
an embroidery of stars emerged,
and old men who bled at Iwo Jima,
dry-eyed youths when the chips were down,
left the tables weeping, collars turned up,
walking out of darkened door-ways
into the remnants of an era,
crooning in the bars their flat laments.
Miners Dean hacked coal with in his youth,
lungs flecked black as sheet-music,
coughed and hummed and reminisced.
In the twilight of his last table,
the air whiskied with smokey shadows,
Jerry still danced like a whacky dervish,
his contorted laughter buckling the air.
Did Sammy's glass eye finally focus,
the tenth cognac simmering like a tune,
the ghost of Dean's son rising from the wreck,
a fatal skid of noise dissolving to song?
As the lights dimmed everything became:
the static and warp of modern music,
rat-packs rapping their gangsta-jazz,
and police cars howling like coyotes,
an arid song-line for the desert.

Urban Fox

A storm the colour of bitter tea
brews above humid alleys.

Silent lightning strides the distance
on gaunt electric legs.

The moon is orange neon,
and the Urban Foxline hums.

On the river, suburban lights
ember like canine eyes.

The storm stirs the vixen too.
A phantom-form raids Council bins.

Antennae-rigged, technicians
bristle like surreal shrubs.

They patrol a grid of city lanes,
the fox's urban paddocks.

There is dog-urine on their boots.
The fox surrounds them with its nose.

A squad from the CSIRO
inspects the glowing infra-red.

In its eerie wash of green heat
they see: a rabbit under floorboards,

a possum drunk on fermented grapes,
punk-rats behind a nightclub.

The fox is uncorroborated,
as longed-for as a rumour.

It conjures a compelling myth.
Strange facts decode from its spoor.

(The radio news reports it fanged
a slow Ferrari on the freeway).

The night is a texture of paradox:
the fox haunts a humid landscape,

pursued in a false terrain,
haunting thickets of pipe and cable.

It fox-dreams a safe clay den,
drizzle and lush stooks by a pond,

scattered hedge-rows and briar,
a sustaining blood on the snow.

The alley walls sweat.
The fox vomits styrene foam.

The Paradoxes of Water:
New and Uncollected Poems 1990–2005

A Lyric on the Natural History of Our Love
For Lyn

Here, memory flares like a goshawk
Rising into the early light.
Our eyes mapped this copper river,
The logic of its fall to the sea,
Scalloped shallows and glinting bream,
Catalogued its grammar of birds:
An inebriation of parrots
Where the sweet pods hung black as wine,
Coughing wattlebirds imbibing;
The jig-sawed peewit's lilting pipe,
Herons roosting the jarrah bridge,
And blue wrens like neon signage,
The river reflecting their light,
(A high day's grand immensity
Structured around such fragile forms);
Kingfishers flashing Persian wings,
Skimming pools tinctured indigo,
And washed in the musk of twilight,
The full-moon's electrolysis
Dissolving stars blue as the birds.
Inland, and the contours displayed
A pattern of market-gardens,
Serried paddocks of strawberries,
The terrain organised like a chart—
Fence grids, gates and rusty byres—
All for the benign purpose of fruit.
There, our picnic was cold Chablis,
The cinnamon of your kisses,
Fresh mangoes and a chicory sky,
Another landscape that framed us.
Gentle gatekeeper of our days,
When the cobalt air conjured clouds
Etched with traceries like marble,
The grain and hue of marri blooms,
You showed me where a limestone bluff

Erupted like a great white whale
From the calm sea of a sand-plain;
Followed an ancient water-course,
Its wetlands glinting like sequins,
Until we emerged on a bluff,
From where we watched the green combers
Fly rainbows on an off-shore wind,
The far deserts breathing seaward,
A day-moon coloured like honey,
The lagoon a lucent jewel.
At low tide night glazed the sand black,
The beach like slick and burnished glass,
A perfect mirror to the stars.
You strolled among the Pleiades,
The Milky Way's misty brilliance,
Your star-flecked hair a constellation,
The beach stippled by galaxies
And the fluorescence of light-years.
These landscapes—texts of earth, river,
Sea and sky—inhabit us still,
Like aquifers of memory,
Intimate as our shared history,
Shaping us with their layered stories—
A pure ecology of our love.

A Homage to the Elephant

They bear their lumber of innocence grandly,
on the grey swaying platforms of their bulk,
drifting the savannah like majestic dhows,
 loaded to their Plimsolls with existence.
Their stumped teak-log legs are paradoxes:
dense with dark tonnage, they articulate
a gait as light and breezy as balsa-wood.
Their flesh, grooved with the grain of ancient rock,
patterned like the rift-valleys of creation,
the plates on which whole continents drift,
folds perfectly over an improbable form.
Theirs is the geometry of large typographies,
and the necessities of heavy haulage.
Cinnamon eyes, jet-lashed and lustred black,
a bird-crest like a Zulu's plumes,
blink small eddies in the African light.
A Sultan's carriage, Hannibal's war cars,
they have seen the mad flesh of human combat,
a bloody marl in the Colosseum,
yet cannot conceive a bullet's trajectory.
They inhabit a century of victims.
Their great brown heads mimic the Nile's delta.
Their language is a pneumatic grammar,
punctuated by body touch and pantomime,
a slow-motion Lambada for the moon,
the lunar aridities of the veldt.
No potentate ever nurtured their children
more gently than a pachyderm fondles its young.
(And Kings have been known to murder a son).
Bones of the dead are caressed like memory.
They are the weighty ponderers of Earth,
a gentle and nomadic inheritance,
like amiable whales who chose to walk the land.
They are mighty sovereigns who justly trumpet.

Construction Site

The scaffolding looms.
Later, riveted with stars,
a steel arch of sky.

Forensic Triptych

EVIDENCE

Who has been climbing
across the sky? Who left that
white thumbprint of dust?

DETENTION

Exfiltrating through
the razor-wire by moonlight—
dreams, exhalations.

POLITICAL CORRECTNESS

In the grim barracks
of his mind each idea
is dipped in acid.

Goat Killing

The white goats in their stony field
look suitably Biblical,

ready to be trussed, their throats
ruptured into warm red grins,

as if the slaughterman quipped,
from his store of Gnostic aphorisms,

did you hear the gag God pulled
on Abraham and his only son?

His smile is a dedicated blade,
flashing through the flesh of words.

Here is death's strange coherence:
a scream of frenzied flies in chorus,

the hard sun like a golden calf,
the goats aptly bewildered.

A day, surreal as an afterlife,
burning in their gaping mouths.

Kosovo

1

Ears, the faintest smile,
nose, from each gaunt face are cut—
Historicism.

2

Crimson horizon,
sunset, bright as a cut throat—
Balkans evening.

from Letters from the Metro

IMPRESSIONS OF THE METRO, FIRST DAY

When I first arrived, an acidulous dark
burnt and stained me like the jet blood of squid.
I sense at once not even the worst life
can prepare one for ennui-after-death.
And then there is portentous old Pluto,
a boring, moon-pale, gross grub of a god,
eyes like rank and dry ebony raisins.
He grins through black teeth as the stile ratchets,
satisfied at his guaranteed quota.
He squats there by his nocturnal river,
the water slow and blue as livid flesh,
a flat and stagnant whiteness for a face.
I can report the notion of sulphur clouds
is a fallacy. Rather, what pervades here
is a stifling smell of acrid loneliness.
Imagine it as a terminal condition,
yet one that never has a releasing end.
A multitude of monads mingle mutely
in eternal solitary confinements,
face-to-face, like bleak and stranded rafts
butting one against the other in thick umbra.
Music's memory and recalled conversations
sear like acid in our sealed and vacant ears.
O for the pure happiness of small semantics,
the delicate and mutual chords of syntax!
Passing gossip would be a deliverance.
Speaking of which, I saw Sartre here today.
He now knows Hell is not other people.
And old Lenin of the wax face thunders
an endless fusillade of baffled silence.
His tongue flutters like a torn May Day flag.
So cherish the gritty edges of noise and voice,
the bouquet and rich wine of dialogue.

[108]

Despise all regimes demanding silence:
the politics of the stopped mouth is death.
Believe me, this null inevitable quiet
gives each moment the texture of forever.

My Daughter Reading

For Chay

My daughter reads in a white hammock,
suspended high in our Cape Lilac.
Its pervasive scent is a sweet mauve smoke
wafting across the yard to where I sit.
It lulls my worry on a gentle breeze,
my anxiety that she might tumble,
tipped from the perch of her green thoughts,
and the day stay indifferent and lovely.
She has chosen an old calico sheet,
slung herself between two sturdy forks,
hauling an encyclopaedia after her.
She has constructed this place carefully,
a paradigm of a child's thinking:
it is hung across a clear half-moon
frosting white in the afternoon.
From there she can watch red wattlebirds
sip the indigo evening and goshawks,
white as salt, hunt geckoes in the scrub,
the sea a blue presence in her imaginings.
(She has seen a unicorn from up there).
Squinting at the emerging flecks of stars,
she queries which one is a planet.
Walking to her I call upwards, asking
the title of the book she ponders.
Tree of Knowledge her smile calls back.
My unease rises with the evening wind.
Later, she climbs down, takes me to safety,
a risk negotiated, a lesson learnt,
moonlight bleaching the shifting sand we tread.

Paradox

A scree of starlight,
the river like jet granite.
Then, a buoyant moon.

Parrots

Lorikeets pattern
the dune heath like a tartan,
raucous as bagpipes.

Premonition

Some days are thorn beds,
the world barbed and wilful,

poison flowers luring
with their fragrant charms.

Birds scratch razor edges
across a glassy lupin sky.

Wind bleeds through the trees
like a dark lament.

And I am a small insect,
fallen on my mottled back.

Stamens of light stab
my sunflower lenses.

I panic that Kafka is God,
that tomorrow I will awake,

a vacuous clerk
in a mildewed room,

scrailing in the air
of this human world.

Remorse

Each night a sentence,
and the moon a manacle
the colour of rust.

A South Perth Dreaming

Along the foreshore's Catherine-wheel rim
the low-rise city cascaded to Mends Street,
blue flukes of starlight stippling Miller's Pond.
The Manning dairy was a clutter of byres,
perched by a harbour of the suburb's past,
where the pig-tailed ghost of a Chinese gardener,
the silt of the Yangtze staining his veins,
tilled the rich serries of marl and loam,
a fire-fly moon white as frangipani.
Heron scrailed by the shimmering river,
their flight like calligraphy on the air.
The Old Mill ticked over time in memory,
and sailed the wind on its wooden kites.
Mysteries of fish flapped on Coode Street jetty,
yellow-fin, bream, cobbler black as night,
parrot fish with flanks spangled in neon.
My grandfather wheezed from World War I
as he cast with artistry into the breeze,
shards of moonlight jagged by a sandbank,
the Kings Park cairn like an apparition
poised in an ether on the river's glaze.
The suburb's jazz was elemental:
a riff of wind through the jacarandas,
the horse-drawn milk-cart's syncopation,
the scat counter-pointing of a bottleo's call
and the mail-man's whistle in the still afternoons,
long bantam choruses just before dawn,
the hum of the highway by the Hurlingham pub.
By day, the slumberous coo and rhythmic billing
of cinnamon doves was the hot noon's pulse,
and mine, as I clambered a pepper tree
up through the sky's delft heights to survey
the sandy grid of my childhood world,
a vista of streets and picket-fence lanes.
In the distance the topaz river blazed,

and the lead-light windows of Douglas Avenue
gulped in the brine of a late sea-breeze,
sounds of the ocean tumbling in the trees.
All this conjured me as a wondering child,
bounded by the river and its mirrorous light,
the founding dream of my neophyte days,
the star-flecked visions of the suburb's nights.

The Moon Over Baghdad

I

The moon over Baghdad
Shines like the tundra –
And the icy drifts
Hold the dead in thrall.
Stars are detonations.

II

The moon over Baghdad
Is a minaret.
It summons phantoms
And hope from the dunes.
The wind is a prayer.

III

The moon over Baghdad
Is a tortured soul.
It glazes the Tigris,
The burden of flesh
It freights to the sea.

IV

The moon over Baghdad
Is gouged from a desert.
Quadrangles of death
Are filled with its rubble—
Mindscapes and mothers.

V

The moon over Baghdad,
Burnished like a sword
From History's scabbard,
Bleeds light blue as blood.
The endless sands imbibe.

The Paradoxes of Water

There is theology in water.
In its pristine and simple atoms,
there are miracles for the lame.
Yet a cripple will submerge,
which is why Lourdes is shallow,
and the climb to it granite-dry.
There are baptisms in its rivers,
the blue cathedrals of its course,
a liquid plunging toward heaven.
A tidal wave is an act of God.
His appetites stretch to whole towns,
which is why insurance agents are pious,
demanding more for floods.
And what could be less lethal
than the fragility of a water drop?
Yet, when marshalled, they break
steel cargoes, bloat the innocent.
Small and constant drips to the skull
crack the mind's struts with echoes.
Water is a chameleon: colourless,
a liquid ether, heraldic with rainbows,
a variegated stellar map,
planets orbiting in its shining lake.
Water can conjure fish from dust,
a stunned frog from beneath gibber:
it will blink at the sodden light,
stony eyes, fractured by the dark,
regaining their watery meniscus,
stinging with the desert's burning blue.
Water can hang in the sky for months,
taunting the savannah from which it came.
Then, conspiring with a burnt sky,
flood the distance with illusion.
Some have gone mad drinking that dream.
In artesian form, cool water

is the secret of a searing waste,
a lagoon deep at the limestone's heart.
Only the most leathery of skinks
and ancient of humans know its taste.
And water, suffusing all delicate life,
is often the chosen means to death:
embracing with lapping silences
those who wade from the heavy tumult,
buoyed and lolled in its weightlessness,
to erode gently by dry moonlight.

The University

Plato's silhouettes
flicker in the lecture hall—
doctrine, agit-prop.

Van Morrison

His golden sax brims
with Celtic moonlight—young Van
croons old Yeats the Blues.

Warder

His tense eyes are like dark key-holes,
and there is metal in his voice.
Life is a set of Standing Orders,
existence, a strip-search to the bone.
Time levels a bead from its tower.

His troublesome child was born
scarred, screaming like a siren.
A suburb from the confinement ward,
he flinched in a yard of sleep.
His sixth sense is for disturbance.

Even small things are portentous:
a mutter of lips, wind at the door,
the codes its whispers, small enigmas,
ravelled secrets in a wall of skulls,
the solipsistic silences.

He dreams a symmetry of corridors,
watches them as they pace, pivoting,
pad, turning on the heels of talk,
framing him in their eyes like mirrors.
He keeps something back: in them, in himself.

Wind

All night the wind's black tumbling,
a scud of stars across the high-rise.
Another mouth gulps air, screaming:
the courtyard spins upwards, surprised.

Morning wheels on gusts of light,
sirens flap from lines like towels,
sparrows break against the brick,
the bay thermals faint brine and clouds.

Old faces peer from mildewed flats.
Like scraps, live birds pirouette.
All night the wind's black tumbling
prepared this morning's silhouette.

Yugoslavia, 1992

Along an ancient front-line
young skulls wait to grin,
their mouths full of moonlight.
A night wind infiltrates, deploys
barbed molecules of apprehension.
At the rim of the Adriatic
granite cracks like shrapnel,
the moon's water magenta red.
From their political barracks,
elders despatch the Minotaurs.
They glint in green armour.
The frontier guards are on alert.
In their gaunt fingers:
the drawn knives of history.